# LET'S TRAVEL

## GRAYSCALE COLORING BOOK FOR ADULTS

*Majestic* **COLORING**

ISBN: 978-1534806771

# FREE DOWNLOAD

**12** FUN DESIGNS FOR YOUR COLORING ENJOYMENT!

**This 'n That Coloring Book for Grown-Ups** is bundled up in one convenient PDF file to download and print at your leisure.

Sign up for our Majestic Coloring mailing list and get a free copy of **This 'n That Coloring Book for Grown-Ups**.

Click here to get started
http://majesticcoloring.com/thisnthat-free

www.ingramcontent.com/pod-product-compliance
Lightning Source LLC
Chambersburg PA
CBHW080603190526

45169CB00007B/2866

*9781534806771*